Every Kid's Guide to
Family Rules and Responsibilities

Written by

JOY BERRY

GROLIER ENTERPRISES INC.
Danbury, Connecticut

About the Author and Publisher

Joy Berry's mission in life is to help families cope with everyday problems and to help children become competent, responsible, happy individuals. To achieve her goal, she has written over two hundred self-help books for children from infancy through age twelve. Her work has revolutionized children's publishing by providing families with practical, how-to, living skills information that was previously unavailable in children's books.

Joy has gathered a dedicated team of experts, including psychologists, educators, child developmentalists, writers, editors, designers, and artists to form her publishing company and to help produce her work.

The company, Living Skills Press, produces thoroughly researched books and audiovisual materials that successfully combine humor and education to teach children subjects ranging from how to clean a bedroom to how to resolve problems and get along with other people.

Managing Editor: Ellen Klarberg
Copy Editors: Kate Dickey
Contributing Editors: Libby Byers, Nancy Cochran, Maureen Dryden,
Yona Flemming, Kathleen Mohr, Susan Motycka
Editorial Assistant: Sandy Passarino

Art Director: Laurie Westdahl
Design: Abigail Johnston, Laurie Westdahl
Production: Abigail Johnston, Caroline Rennard
Illustrations designed by: Bartholomew
Inker: Rashida Tessler
Colorer: Rashida Tessler
Composition: Curt Chelin

Wherever there are two or more people, it is important to have rules. A family consists of two or more people. Therefore, it is important for families to have rules.

In **EVERY KID'S GUIDE TO FAMILY RULES AND RESPONSIBILITIES** you will learn about the following:

- family rules,
- family meetings,
- categories of family rules,
- consequences of breaking rules, and
- family responsibilities.

R*ules* are the guidelines that tell people how to act and what to do.

Spoken rules are rules that are talked about and agreed upon by the people who must follow them.

Unspoken rules are rules that are not talked about and agreed upon. However, the people who must follow them usually know that the rules exist.

Spoken rules are usually more effective than unspoken ones.

It is easier for people to understand rules that they have talked about. People are more likely to follow rules they understand.

It is difficult for people to understand rules that they have not talked about. People are less likely to follow rules they do not understand.

It is important for people in a family to talk with each other if family rules are to be spoken instead of unspoken.

Family members can talk to each other individually. They can also talk to each other in a group.

A get-together where family members discuss family matters is called a *family meeting.*

These meetings can take place regularly. They can take place once a week, or they can take place once a month. Family meetings can also take place whenever there is a need for one.

Positive things can be accomplished during family meetings if family members follow eight basic guidelines.

Guideline 1. Family meetings need to be scheduled at a time when every family member can attend.

Family meetings should not be scheduled when any family member has something important to do.

Guideline 2. Distractions that might take a family member's attention away from a family meeting need to be avoided.

Here are some ways to avoid possible distractions:

- Put a note on the front door of the house that reads, "Family meeting in progress. Do not disturb."
- Unplug the telephone.
- Turn off the TV.
- Discourage family members from bringing items such as books, toys, portable radios, or tape recorders to family meetings.
- Invite only family members to family meetings.

Guideline 3. It helps to have an agenda for every family meeting.

An agenda is a list of subjects that are to be discussed during a meeting.

It is a good idea for every family member to help decide what subjects should be included on the agenda.

Important subjects should be put at the top of the agenda, and the less important subjects should be put at the bottom.

Guideline 4. Before a family meeting begins, everyone needs to decide when it will end.

All family members should help end the meeting at that time.

Subjects that have not been discussed before the meeting ends can be put on the agenda for the next family meeting.

Guideline 5. It helps to have one family member lead the family meeting.

The same person can lead every family meeting, or family members can take turns leading meetings.

It is the job of the person who leads a family
meeting to
- organize the agenda,
- begin the meeting on time,
- make sure each subject on the agenda is discussed
  and resolved, and
- end the meeting on time.

Guideline 6. It is best when every family member participates in each family meeting.

Family members should be allowed to share their thoughts and feelings about each subject on the agenda.

The thoughts and feelings that are shared should never be ignored or put down. Instead, they should be given attention and respected.

Guideline 7. Family meetings need to be conducted in an orderly manner.

To make sure a meeting does not get out of control, family members need to

- cooperate with the person who is leading the meeting,
- take turns talking,
- give their full attention to the person who is talking, and
- avoid interrupting the person who is talking.

Guideline 8. The decisions that are made in a family meeting need to be approved by the parents in the family.

Parents are responsible for the overall safety and well-being of every family member. This responsibility entitles them to the ultimate control over family matters.

It is best when parents and children agree on the family decisions that are made. However, it is not likely that this will happen all the time.

It is good when children in a family express their opinions. It is also good when parents consider their children's opinions. But regardless of what their children think, parents must do what they think is best.

Every family is different. Every family needs to make its own rules. There are six categories that need to be considered when families are making their rules.

Category 1. Rules About Space

It is important for families to have rules about space.

Rules about space tell family members
- what areas in and around the home are OK to be in,
- what areas in and around the home are off limits,
- what activities can and cannot be done in certain areas, and
- where family members can and cannot go when they leave home.

Category 2. Rules About Time

It is important for families to have rules about time.

Rules about time tell family members
- when things happen (the family schedule),
- when certain things should be finished, and
- when certain things can and cannot be done.

Category 3. Rules About Family Possessions

It is important for families to have rules about possessions.

Rules about possessions tell family members
- what each person owns,
- what owners can and cannot do with their things,
- how to borrow and return things, and
- what must be done when someone's things are lost, abused, or broken by another family member.

Category 4. Rules About Work

It is important for families to have rules about work.

FAMiLY WoRK CHART

CASEY	EMPTY THE TRASH	EVERY TUE./THUR.
	DRY THE DISHES	EVERY OTHER WEEK
	SET THE TABLE	EVERY OTHER WEEK
	MAKE BED AND CLEAN ROOM	EVERY DAY
	MOW THE LAWN WEED THE GARDEN	EVERY OTHER SAT.
	VACUUM AND DUST HOUSE	EVERY OTHER SAT.
ANNiE	FEED THE DOG/CAT	EVERY DAY
	DRY THE DISHES	EVERY OTHER WEEK
	SET THE TABLE	EVERY OTHER WEEK
	MAKE BED AND CLEAN ROOM	EVERY DAY

Rules about work tell family members
- who is supposed to work,
- what work needs to be done,
- when the work needs to be done, and
- where the work needs to be done.

Category 5. Rules About Play

It is important for families to have rules about play.

Rules about play tell family members
- who is OK to play with,
- what is healthy and safe to play with,
- when it is healthy and safe to play, and
- where it is healthy and safe to play.

Category 6. Rules About Family Habits and Customs

It is important for families to have rules about habits and customs.

Rules about habits and customs tell family members
- what they will do during time spent together,
- what they will do for vacations, holidays, and special events, and
- how often certain practices will be repeated.

It is important that every family rule has a consequence. A *consequence* is what can happen to a person who does not follow a rule. Usually it is a logical penalty or a punishment.

Most often, people want to obey the rules because they do not want to experience the consequences of breaking the rules.

People who break a rule must be prepared to suffer the consequence. They have no one to blame but themselves for the penalty they must pay or the punishment they must experience.

In addition to making rules and establishing consequences, it is important for families to assign responsibilities to family members. A *responsibility* is something that needs to be done.

Here are some responsibilities of family members:

Someone in the family must earn the money for the family to use.

Someone must also
- shop for the things that the family needs and
- pay the money that the family owes. (This is sometimes called paying the bills.)

Someone in the family must

- take care of any babies or small children in the family and
- take care of any pet the family might own.

Someone must also
- prepare the food for the family to eat,
- organize and clean the place where the family lives, and
- launder the clothes the family wears.

Someone in the family must
- take care of the outside of the house, including any yard or garden the family might have, and
- clean and take care of any cars the family might own.

Someone must also see that the family possessions which break or stop working are repaired or replaced.

It is not good for one family member to take on most of the responsibilities. It is not fair to the person who is doing everything. It is not good for the people who are letting the one person do everything.

It is best when the family responsibilities are divided among the family members. When this happens, everyone does something so that no one person has to do everything.

Everyone can feel good because he or she is making a contribution, and no one will feel abused.

It is a good idea for families to put into writing the decisions they make about rules, consequences, and responsibilities.

It is also a good idea to put this list in a place where every family member can see it so these decisions will not be forgotten or misunderstood by family members in the future. Families who are respectful of their well-defined rules and responsibilities will most likely produce happy and healthy family members.